Acknowledgements

The photographs of the family featured in this book
are posed by models. Many thanks to the Cook
family for their help in the making of this book.

The authors and publisher would also like to thank:
the Prison Service Headquarters, the staff and
inmates of HMP Guys Marsh and the
Sussex Police Service.

All photographs by Zul Mukhida.
Illustrations by Clare Heronneau.

First published 1999 by
A & C Black (Publishers) Ltd
35 Bedford Row, London WC1R 4JH.

ISBN 0-7136-5094-X

© 1999 Sandra Cain and Margaret Speed.

A CIP catalogue record for this book
is available from the British Library.

Typeset in 14/16 Stone by Judith Gordon.

Printed in Hong Kong through Colorcraft Ltd.

Dad's in Prison

Sandra Cain and Margaret Speed
Photographs by Zul Mukhida

A & C Black · London

I'm Simon and this is my brother Mark.
Last year our Dad was sent to prison.
This is the story of what happened.

One morning a police car pulled up outside our house
and two police officers got out.

I wondered what they were doing and called Mum
to look out of the window.

I couldn't believe it when I saw the police officers walking up to our door. We heard a loud knock. Dad let the officers in. One of them arrested Dad and said, 'You do not have to say anything, but it may harm your defence if you do not mention when questioned something which you later may rely on in court.'

The officer went on, 'Anything you do say may be given in evidence against you.'

I'd heard the words before on television, but it was a shock to hear them being said to my dad.

Dad said he had to go to the police station with the officers. He told us not to worry, but we felt scared.

That night Mark needed a lot of cuddles from Mum.
He was worried that she might go away as well.

When we found out that Dad was going to be sent to prison, Mark and I were very sad. Mum told us that we would be able to visit Dad in prison and that he would be writing to us soon.

A few days later, Dad's letter arrived.

Inside the envelope was a special piece of paper called a visiting order. It had Dad's name and prison number on it. Mum told us it was like a ticket which allowed us into the prison to visit Dad.

Mark and I couldn't wait to see him again,
but we felt nervous too. What would the prison be like?

That evening Dad phoned. We all spoke to him
and I got an extra long turn. I told Dad that we really
missed him. 'Be brave and look after Mum and Mark
for me,' he said. Dad told me that the prison was a long
way from home. The coach journey would take nearly
three hours.

The day of the visit arrived. We had to get up
early to catch the coach. It was full of other people
going to the prison and felt hot and stuffy.
We were glad when the journey ended.

I was really surprised when I saw the prison
for the first time. It looked more like a school
or an office, with flowers at the front.

But as we walked towards the entrance
we could see razor wire fencing all around the walls
and bars on the windows. I began to feel nervous
and wondered what it was like to be locked up like Dad.

All the visitors had to queue up outside the
door of the prison. We were first in line, but
we had to wait for nearly twenty minutes
before we were allowed to go inside.

Once we were inside the prison, Mum handed in our visiting order to a prison officer.

Then we had to queue again until it was our turn to be searched. Mum explained that all visitors to the prison have to be searched for weapons. A second prison officer pressed a button on the wall and some glass doors opened automatically. We walked through the doors and they shut behind us.

We were in a narrow room with rows of lockers in it and a large screen at one end. Mum had to stand in front of the screen and lift her arms in the air while the prison officer switched on a metal detector and moved it over her body.

The detector made a high-pitched screeching noise. Mark didn't like the noise, but the lady told him not to worry. When it was my turn to be scanned I thought it was fun.

The prison officer told us that we were not allowed
to take anything in with us into the visits room.
She asked Mum to put her bag in the locker.
Mark's Panda Bear had to be locked away too.

Mark thought he might never see it again
and wanted to cry. 'It's alright,' the prison officer told him,
'when the visit to your dad is over, we'll let Panda Bear
out and you can take him home.'

We were taken into a huge room with rows
and rows of tables and chairs. We were told to sit
at table number 12 and wait for Dad.

Before long we saw Dad coming into the room
through a different door. I was so happy to see him again,
but I thought he looked strange in his prison uniform.
We all hugged and kissed. Dad made a big fuss of Mark.

A prison officer walked around the visits room with a dog. Dad told us that it was a sniffer dog, and its job was to search for drugs. Mark stared at the big bunch of keys hanging from the officer's belt. 'I wonder if those are the keys that are used to lock Dad up,' he whispered to me.

The visits room was crowded and noisy
with lots of children running around.
There was the sound of people laughing
and I could hear people crying too.
Mum bought us drinks from the prison
canteen and we told Dad all our news.

Mum and Dad seemed to have a lot
to talk about. After a while I got bored,
so I took Mark over to the play area
and watched television for a bit
while Mark played on the slide.

The visit lasted two hours.
The time seemed to go very quickly.
A prison officer came up to us and said,
'Finish your visit now, please.'

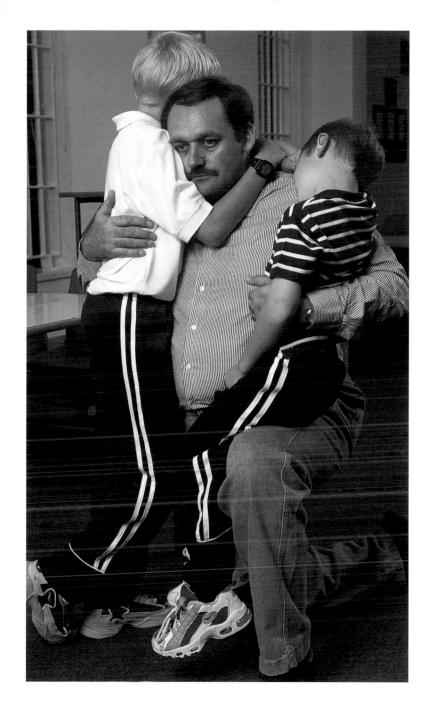

Mark and I both got upset when we cuddled Dad goodbye. We felt really bad about going home without him.

'Don't cry, boys,' Dad said. 'I'll see you again in two weeks and I'll write as often as I can.'

Mum cried too when
it was time to leave.
She and Dad kissed
each other for a
long, long time.

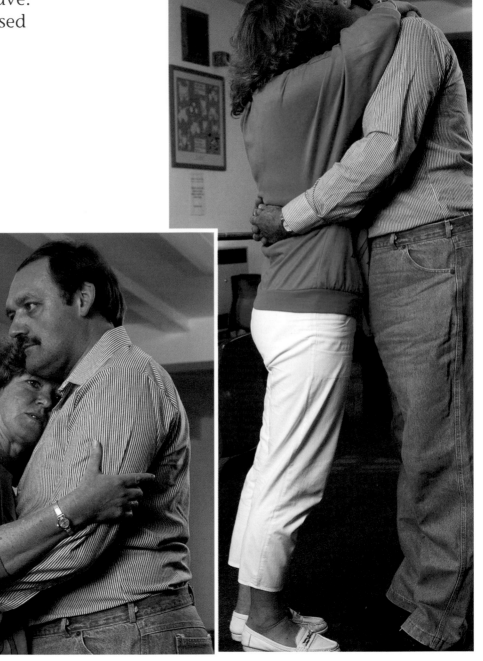

The prison officer was waiting by the lockers.
She unlocked Panda Bear and gave him to Mark.
Mark was very glad to have his bear back.
He didn't want to leave him to be locked up like Dad.

We got on the coach again for the long journey home.
We didn't talk much. We were all too tired and felt sad
to have left Dad behind.

It was very late when we arrived back home.
Mark took Panda Bear up to bed and fell asleep
straight away.

Next morning Mark and I sat in the kitchen and wrote letters to Dad. We told him how good it had been to see him, and how much we loved him. We sent him some photos of ourselves and Mark sent him some pictures which he'd painted at school. We hoped Dad would be able to pin them up on his cell wall.

Dear Dad,
It was great seeing you last week. Hope you are ok. I was in Cub papers the other day, I was the old Charester. Here is a picture of a front cover of my topic book, the sheep I felt like drawing picture of you.
Hope you come out soon.

Dear DaD,
I Loved seing you. I am sending you a cord and I hope you come out soon.
Love from
Simon

Dad wrote to us every week
and told us about the different things
he was doing in prison.

In replying to this letter, please write on the envelope:
Number. DM.442.1 Name. John Smith

G (3) Wing
H.M.P. Dale Garden,
BRINSWOOD,
Redland
RD64 5PQ

Dear Simon and Mark,
    Thank you for your last letter.
I am glad that you are both getting on
well at school. I am OK too.
    The prison garden has lots of
flowers and one of my jobs is to look
after them. I am also learning how to use
the computer in the prison classroom so I'll
be able to help you with your homework
when I come home. I borrow books
from the prison library which I enjoy
reading in my cell. Sometimes I even
help with the cooking in the prison
kitchen.

Tell Mum I shall write her a separate letter. Be good boys and help Mum in the house.
I am making you both a special present. It'll be in the arts and craft room. It'll be ready for your next visit. I love you very much and I am looking forward to seeing you next week.

Love Dad
x x x

23

We decided to tell our friends what had happened to Dad.
Everyone wanted to know what it's like inside a prison and
what we'd seen when we visited Dad.

My friend Joe wondered what it's like being a prisoner.
'Dad says the worst thing about prison is being locked up
and losing your freedom and not being able to be with
your family and friends,' I told him.

'Dad says the letters he gets from us are really important to him. We write to him every week.'

'When's your dad going to be free?' Joe wanted to know. 'When he finishes his prison sentence,' I said.

'I bet you'll be glad when he comes home,' said Joe.
'Too right,' I said. 'Although Dad used to tell us off sometimes, we really miss him.' Then Mark cheered us up. He told Joe, 'Mum says that when Dad comes home we're going to have a big party to celebrate!'